From the Girls Next Door:

Taking a STEP in the Right Direction

Erika Hill, MS, LAPC, NCC

Jamilah Jones, MS, LAC, NCC

The advice and strategies found within may not be suitable for every situation. This work is sold with the understanding that neither of the authors is held responsible for the results accrued from the advice in this book.

Book cover designed by Terrance Hill Jr.

ISBN 978-1-0918-8862-3

First paperback edition April 2018

Published by S.T.E.P.S. Counseling & Consulting
www.stepscounselingconsulting.com

I want to dedicate this book to my Ladybug, mommy, daddy, stepmommy, my love Michael, grandparents, aunties, uncles, cousins, godparents, godbrothers and godsisters, godchildren, my besties, and my amazing friends that I have been blessed with. I will forever be grateful for my strong support system.

-Jamilah Jones, MS, LAC, NCC

I dedicate this book to my wonderful husband, Terrance. Thank you for your unconditional love and support. My daughter, Kylie and son, Terrance, thank you for being my motivation. My parents, mother in love Danielle, my siblings, nephews, nieces, family, and friends. Thank you for being an amazing support system.

-Erika Hill, MS, LAPC, NCC

From the Girls Next Door: *Yes, I Am Single with No Kids. So What?*

Somewhere it must have been written that you should be married by a certain age, and if not married, you should at least be in a relationship. And there must also be a paragraph about having kids by a certain age. Apparently, I missed that memo, and to tell you the truth, I'm not mad about that. You shouldn't be mad if you missed that memo, either. Timing is everything, and when it is your time it will happen.

Time to Speak the Truth:

Deep down inside you're feeling ready to settle down, but you work hard on trying not to think about that too much. Unfortunately, social media constantly reminds you. Your aunt asks you at every holiday event about the ex you brought to meet the family at the last event, knowing the family already gossiped about your break up. And every time you compliment a parent on how cute their child is, they respond by asking "So, when are you having yours?" You basically can't get a break from your reality; the reality that you have not chosen, but have accepted.

Now What?

You're frustrated with the constant reminders about your single life, but you have to put on a fake smile and act like you're happy being single and that marriage and kids are nowhere near your mind. Or, maybe you feel like you have to let everyone know you're ready to settle down. You may be throwing hints to any and everyone who will listen to you. You keep putting it out there, because you're ready for the universe to give you what you been asking for.

Go Time!

Don't let society dictate your timing. What is meant for you will happen for you. Enjoy the single life and enjoy this time with you. The last thing you want is to become so desperate that you end up settling for someone who doesn't make you truly happy; or worse, to end up being only a "baby mama" when your goal was to become a wife.

At the same time, you have to ask yourself why ARE you still single? Sometimes it can simply be that you haven't met 'the one.' Other times it could be that you've not switched up your

3

pattern in the guys you choose to date. What kind of men are you dating? Are you ignoring the signs they reveal in the beginning just so you can say you're in a relationship? Are you going places where you might meet someone new? It's okay to try that new restaurant by yourself or with friends. Stop going to the same "poppin" happy hour spot. Try the other happy hour spot downtown. FYI, it's 2018. You can sign up for online dating. The point I'm trying to make is that change is good, and timing is everything.

From the Girls Next Door: *Strength, A Gift and a Curse*

People often commend your strength. Other people tell you they admire your strength, and they wish they there strong like you. If you are like me, you pray for strength and thank God for your strength. However, there is those other times. Those times when you really don't feel that strong. Those times when you want to be vulnerable. Don't be afraid to admit it…. are times when you ask God why he selected you to be the strong one. I know, we are hypocrites. Unfortunately, life causes us to be hypocrites at times.

Time to Speak the Truth:

Being strong requires you to have to deal with obstacles you did not have time to prepare for. Being strong requires you to be the person people emotionally depend on. Being strong requires you to be the person with all the answers. Being strong requires you to be the person that always have their shit together. Now because you present yourself in such a manner, you have to appear to always have it together. So now when you want to cry on someone's shoulder, you have to cry to yourself at night as you squeeze your pillow. Then you have to wake up in the morning and face the world, and act like you did not cry yourself to sleep last night.

Now what?

You are becoming overwhelmed with your being so strong. You want to be on the opposite side of the table for once. You want to take a break from everyone depending on you, and you don't want to seem like you are being mean. You want to be vulnerable for a minute, but you don't want to seem weak. You want people to know you don't know all the answers, but you don't want to seem dumb. The reality of it all, is that you don't want a break forever. You just want a break for a few minutes. So now you have to figure out to be on the other side of the table and still remain the strong person you know you are.

Go Time!

Put yourself first!!! You cannot pour from an empty cup. You cannot be emotionally available for everyone, when you are not even emotionally available. It is ok to put your phone on "Do Not Disturb". Sometimes you have to take a break from the outside world, because the world can drain you. It is okay to call a confidant and cry and/or talk. If you don't have anyone you can confide in but you are that person everyone confides in, then we have a problem. In the meantime, if you do not have anyone to confide in, write it in a journal and/or contact a counselor. Speaking to a counselor or a therapist does not make you crazy or weak. It is just another strategy used to help you organize your emotions. If you don't know the answer to something, admit it. People respect honesty. Most importantly, remember....it is okay, not to be okay. Just be honest about what you are feeling, but just own it. When you own your emotions, no one can throw it in your face. Now don't mistake this for telling any and everyone what you are going through. I will

never promote telling your business to everyone.

However, I am saying it is okay to be

transparent. Queen, your crown is so sturdy that

when you bend your head down to cry, your crown

will not fall off!!!

From the Girls Next Door: *Single Mothers' Club*

As a single mother, you don't give yourself enough credit. You spend so much time having to hold it all down and make it happen for your children, that you seldom realize how hard you work for your family all by yourself. You don't see that you're the mother, father, doctor, teacher, maid (at least that's what the kids make you feel like from time to time), and whatever else your child needs you to be. You are the sole provider of it all and for everyone around you. This chapter is for you. This chapter is to help you realize that you are bomb.com and that it's time to focus on YOU.

Time to Speak the Truth:

I have many friends who are single mothers by choice, and some not by choice. I look at them with admiration, because I see their struggle. Their days are never-ending. After work, school, or sometimes both, they still have to go home and put on their mother hat. They are unable to ask someone else to put the kids in the bath or help with homework. They are unable to have someone else cook dinner or iron clothes for the next day. Let's not forget they are also unable to split the monthly bills. Everything relies totally on them, and single mothers do it all by themselves. They do not do it for an award but because their children depend on them, and they have no choice but to get it done. A lot of single mothers are so used to being unable to depend on others that they've become subconsciously trained to get it done by themselves. Single mothers are superheroes that do not even realize their superpowers. Though this independent mentality has instilled an undeniable strength within single mothers, many forget to celebrate themselves and focus on what is next for them.

Now What?

Being a single mother is hard as hell, but guess what Sis, you are doing it! You are doing it all to make sure your children are happy and at peace. You are doing it all on your own, and you're doing a damn good job! Nevertheless, when is the last time you did something for you? You go so hard for your family that you tend to forget about your own needs. You've built a box for your family, but have you ever gone outside of the box to do something different for you? Just like you reward your kids, when is the last time you rewarded yourself? You do things to make your children smile, but when is the last time you did something to make yourself smile?

Go Time!

If you answered any of those questions with "it's been a long time" or even a "damn, I can't remember," then this chapter is for you. This chapter is meant for you to realize that you need to do something for YOU from time to time. You go so damn hard that you don't even realize it until someone else brings it to your attention. Well, Sis, here is your reminder that you are doing the damn thing! Pat yourself on the back.. and then go do something for YOU. You deserve it, girl!

13

From the Girls Next Door: *School and Work Have Become Too Much*

I often question myself, asking what the hell I was thinking when I decided to go back for my Ph.D. In fact, I asked myself that same damn question when I was getting my master's. Now that I think about it, I think I asked myself that question when I was getting my bachelor's. No, I've never asked myself that question because I didn't see the purpose of continuing my education, because, trust me…I am all for education. I asked myself that question because it can become overwhelming, trying to maintain a full-time job while working toward a degree.

Time to Speak the Truth:

This shit is too much. Point, blank,

period! How are you supposed to figure out what

to make a priority? I'm sick of people telling me I

'just' need time management skills. Oh, and let's

not even talk about what it's like if you have a

child or children, and/or a partner, not to mention,

a dog that needs to be fed and walked daily. On top

of that, I have to make sure I stay on top of my

responsibilities at work, because I need my job. I

can't call out to get my work done because I need

to save my days for when I am really sick or in

some cases when my child is sick. To be all the

way honest, I need to save my days for when I

need to take a real vacation, so I can practice that

self-care thing everyone always preaches about. In

some instances, people don't even have paid time

off. So how is it possible for a woman to be successful in school, work, and in her personal life?

Now What?

You're trying to figure out if you should just quit school. Then you realize that would mean you'll have to pay back those loans quicker than you anticipated. That may be one of the reasons you decided to go back to school to begin with! Even though going back to school required you to apply for more loans, it pushed back the due date of your loan. You can't quit your job, because you came too far to give up now; you have too many people looking up to you and depending on you. You know you need the financial boost an additional degree would provide. So, the bottom line is, you have more to lose than gain by giving up on school.

Go Time!

I don't care if you're in your first semester or in your last semester, giving up is not an option. Remember why you started. No one said it was going to be easy. If it was easy, everyone would have their master's. Everyone would be walking around with Dr. in front of his or her name. School is only temporary, but this accomplishment will last forever. Stay a little longer at work to get that assignment done. Get up and go to the library to avoid distractions, remain focused, and get it done. It's okay to bring your laptop to your son's basketball game. Go right ahead and type and cheer at the same time! Do what you have to do to get it done. Just keep this in mind, still find time for you. (Don't roll your eyes, and don't let me lose you right here). When people think about time for themselves, they think about a seven-day vacation or a whole Sunday at the spa, which everyone can use and would be amazing to be able to do; but the reality is it cannot be done right now. I'm talking about those little breaks that add up. When was the last time you went out for lunch, and not at your desk? Take the long way home every once in a while, to spend a few extra minutes in the car alone. Wake up a 15 mins earlier to meditate. Do whatever it takes to avoid that overwhelmed feeling. You'll be less stressed when it's time to study and/or type that paper. I'm not saying you'll feel less stressed every time, but certainly more times than you have been feeling lately. When you graduate, you'll realize it was all worth it. Then make sure you treat yourself to that spa and/or vacation you have been wanting to go on.

From the Girls Next Door: *My Dreams Seem So Far Away*

I know I work hard. I know I've been patient. I know I've been networking. So, why has "it" not happened for ME?!? "It" being my dream job, that promotion, a grant for that business, that big performance; that one thing that will make me feel like my career dreams are actually happening. It just seems like time is passing, and things are not getting any easier. I know they say anything worth having doesn't come easy, but how much harder can it really get? How much sleep do I have to lose? How much more praying do I have to do?

Time to Speak the Truth:

Boy, do I know this feeling. To me, the feeling is even worse when you finally think that big break is about to happen and then your future says, "Just kidding! I'm joking! Not ready!" Since we ARE speaking the truth, I think I need to tell you about my recent experience with this exact feeling. Everything was lining up for me. I built up my confidence to apply to take a big exam that would help me in my future. I consistently studied for about six weeks. The week of, I took a bunch of pre-tests. (I always do well on those pre-tests!) So now I felt really ready. Usually, on days like that one I listen to gospel to build up my nerves and soothe my spirit. This time, though, I felt like I needed my "hype" music. In the past things did not always go the way I wanted them to go, but I knew that this time I had it. So, on my way to take the test, I had Cardi B's song, "Get Up 10," on replay.

This was my 10. I was ready. I wasn't taking any more losses. I sat in front of that computer, I said my prayers, I read the first question, and said, "God damn." I was no longer hyped, my nerves came back, and I told myself to be prepared for another loss. Then I hyped myself up again, and reminded myself of who I was. I sat up straight and gave it my all. I completed the exam and went to the front to get the paper that would tell me whether I had passed or failed. And guess what?!? The paper said FAILED. Not only did I fail, I failed by FOUR QUESTIONS. How hard did I cry? Talk about heartbroken. Then to keep it all the way 100, I felt a sense of embarrassment. I had so many people rooting for me. I then had to turn around and tell them all that I had FAILED.

Now What?

Was this a sign that I should be doing something else? Maybe I should give up. Maybe they were right when they said my business would never be successful. LIES, LIES, and more LIES!!! Who cares what people said. Who cares that I failed that exam. Who cares that things were taking longer than expected. What was I going to do? Quit and be left with a whole lot of woulda, shouda, coulda? So, I told myself, if you got over the last disappointment, what the hell makes you think you won't get over this one? I understand that you're tired. We're all tired! One thing I can tell you for sure...it will all be worth it in the end. Each day that you wake up is another opportunity to perfect your craft.

I would highly suggest that you do a self-reflection and think about the strategies you have used in the past. Then, stop using the ones that aren't working. You can have the same goal, just with different strategies. You also need the self-reflection to make sure that your career dream is really what you want. I'm not asking you to second guess yourself because of a few mishaps that occurred while working on your dreams. During a sermon titled, "Death of Your Last Dream," Pastor Michael Walrond Jr. spoke about creating dreams to prove a point to people. Don't focus on a dream simply to prove you can actually achieve it and be successful at it. Don't focus on a dream because someone else told you that you should do it. Your dream should be something you are passionate about. Don't create a dream because you want the attention you see other people receive when they're doing what you are dreaming of doing. Your dream should fill your spirit; it should be the missing part you feel you need to complete you.

Go Time!

Now that you've self-reflected and realized what works and what doesn't work, it's time to get to work. It's time to prove to yourself that you can accomplish your goals and make your dreams come true. While working, remember to work in silence. Don't work in silence because you aren't sure who really wishes you well (which is another topic), but also to avoid making the mistake of having to tell people that you failed, which then becomes a constant reminder to yourself. I'm not saying you should be ashamed of your failures, though. In fact, I'm telling you to NEVER be ashamed of your failures. But don't talk about what you're doing until you're comfortable with sharing that information. You're the person who should be in control of your destiny and make the decisions about how you want to handle things.

Remember: Anything worth having is worth fighting for. You may not get up at 10, like Cardi B said; or even 11. In fact, you may not get up until the 33rd count. But truth be told, none of that matters. What matters is that you got up!

From the Girls Next Door: *Maintaining a Long-Distance Relationship*

So, you meet someone, and you exchange numbers. Through conversation you realize that you don't live in the same city; or, you may not even live in the same state. Hell, you may even be in different countries. Who knows, one of you may be in the army. Either way, it's long-distance. This may make you a little hesitant about taking the relationship seriously. You don't see a point in taking it any further. You may be contemplating ending what you've started, because you don't see a point in it at all. But to your surprise, as much as you don't see a point in it and want to end it, you just can't seem to stop communicating with this person. The connection in undeniable. It's just like, "Damn. Why do you have to live so far away?"

Time to Speak the Truth:

You couldn't trust the last person you were with, and you only lived 15 minutes away from each other. Shit! To be all the way honest, you couldn't even trust the person you were with before that, and you lived together! So, how the hell can you trust a person who lives thousands of miles from you? For one, you know, people have their sexual needs. And you also know you can't be there to fulfill those sexual desires when they are in need, because they are so far away. If you're real with yourself, you'll admit you aren't only worried about them; you're worried about yourself, too! Some of you may be holding off on having sex until marriage or until the time is right. In that case, a long-distance relationship can definitely contribute to building a strong foundation through communication. Realistically, a relationship shouldn't be based on sex; sex is just the icing on the cake! So, let's discuss the other attributes that can affect a long-distance relationship. Sometimes you just want to be in the presence of your significant other. You just want to sit and talk to him or her in person and not through FaceTime. You want to be able to hold his or her hand and smell the fragrance of him or her. Oh, I know! Trust me, I do!

Now What?

So, you find yourself in the long-distance relationship you thought you'd never be in. You find yourself counting down the days until you can see your boo again. You're wondering if he misses you as much as you miss him. You're sending him random texts so he knows you miss him and are thinking about him. You even send some pictures every now and then. What type of pictures? Now THAT is all up to you! (Just try to remember that you should not have your face in the picture if it's one that shows more than what you would want someone other than your boo to see.) You're planning an agenda for the next time you see each other. You're still wondering how much longer you can handle this long-distance thing. You're still wondering if it's worth it.

Go Time!

Let it flow! If your significant other is

communicating with you as much as you want and need, then it's worth it. Being in a long-distance relationship taught me the importance of communication. It actually forced me to communicate. My previous relationship made me feel like communication wasn't that serious, because I felt like my feelings weren't important. Being in a long-distance relationship taught me that if someone is interested in you, they'll put in the work to show that you're worth the effort of maintaining the relationship. But you must be willing to put in the work also. The best part is, every time you see each other there is so much excitement behind it, because it's like a vacation for at least one of you. You get to show each other the various sights, local attractions, and restaurants where you each live. As time goes by, and you realize you're in this for the long run, it will be time to figure out who is going to move. That can be a difficult conversation, but it will eventually have to happen if you are discussing a future together. So, focus less on the distance apart, and focus more on how happy you are despite the distance. I'm not saying it's easy, because Lord knows I miss my baby. The hardest part is when it's time to leave each other. And if there's been a disagreement of some kind, it's even more difficult. That's when FaceTime is your best friend. However, I can honestly say that I am living with no regrets. Timing is everything, and we are taking it one day at a time. You know he must be one hell of a person if he can keep a smile on MY face from miles away! That goes for your significant other as well. If you are smiling while thinking about him as you read this, distance should not stop you from allowing the relationship to blossom.

From the Girls Next Door: *It is Absolutely Okay to Say No*

Are you that person everyone comes to because they know the word "no" is not in your vocabulary? They know that if they need to borrow something, they can depend on you. They know that if they need someone to go with them somewhere, they can call on you. They know that if they need any type of favor, you're the person to call. Even though you're tired, you still find the energy to go or do. Lending money is not in your budget this week, but you will find a way to do that if someone needs help. You actually feel bad any time you have to say no. Being that dependable person is a gift and a curse. And for me lately, it has been feeling more like a curse.

Time to Speak the Truth:

If you are single and/or do not have any kids, people don't understand how you could ever have the audacity to tell them "No." They seem to think that if you're single and/or don't have any kids, you have all the time and money in the world. If you are married and/or have kids, people tend to not even take that into consideration. They still think they can ask you for whatever, whenever. They don't realize that you are muthafuckin tiyad! Not just plain old tired; you are tiyad!! You are completely over people asking you for anything. You don't want to go anywhere with anybody. You actually want to have a lazy day to yourself. You definitely don't want to lend out any more money, because you rarely get it back, and you

35

know you can't afford to lend money that you won't ever get back. Nevertheless, you are just simply tiyad! Truth be told, you are really over everyone and everything, because it seems like YOU can't ask anybody for anything. The crazy part is, you rarely ask anyone for anything as it is. And when you do ask, you don't always get the response you're hoping for. It seems like you just don't get back what you put out. And all of this is just making you tiyad. The reality is, you are tiyad of the habit you started! People only do what you allow them to do.

Now What?

You are tiyad, but you still have a soft spot for your loved ones. You hate saying "No," especially when you understand they really need you. You also realize you're basically putting everyone else's needs before your own. You want to be able to help; but you feel like everyone has drained you of all the help you have in you. You also just do not know how to say, "No." That is one word that is not in your vocabulary when it comes to the people you love. So now you are torn between choosing yourself or them.

Go Time!

When YOU ask people for something, they don't seem to have any problem telling you, "No." And when they do, you're annoyed for the moment, but that moment passes, and you're over it. Honestly, there are some people you wouldn't even dare to ask because you know they will either say "No" or later throw it back in your face. (Don't you hate people like that?!?) Anyway, do not love those people any less. They say "No" because they cannot give you what they do not have; and no can pour from an empty cup. You cannot continue to over-exhaust yourself. If your friends and family love and care about you the way you love and care about them, they should understand that if you say "No" you really don't have it, or you just cannot do it. Start saying, "No!" Let's practice saying it together. "NO! N-O! NO!" And when the time comes that you actually have to say it, don't feel bad. Now, I am not telling you to begin saying "No" just to be mean. I am telling you to say "No" because what they are asking of you is inconvenient for you. Do what you can, when you can. Keywords: WHEN YOU CAN. You can no longer put everyone else's needs before yours. I don't care if you are single, married, have kids, or do not have kids. You are a priority. You matter. Right now, this very moment, I challenge you to put yourself first.

From the Girls Next Door: *It is Okay to Outgrow A Friendship*

Before writing this chapter, I had to meditate, thinking about all of the friendships I have had in my life in order to truly be honest about this topic. And, the answer I came up with in the end is, "Hell yeah. It's okay to outgrow a friendship." In fact, it's sometimes downright necessary. Out of respect for your own peace of mind and where you are in life, some people may no longer fit in with the lifestyle you are trying to create for yourself; or, they may have shown you that they do not want to fit in with where you are going in life. As the old folks used to say, some friends are only meant for a season while other friendships last a lifetime.

Time to Speak the Truth:

Outgrowing a friendship feels like all the other growing pains in life. The shit hurts. You think of the memories (mostly the good times), and somehow you have to remind yourself of the bad times to validate your growth decision. Trust me, I have done it, too. It hurts to let a friendship go, especially if it was someone you were loyal to. However, as I've gotten older, I've come to realize and accept that some friendships which were meant to be outgrown change as your life goes in new directions. I didn't have an alert that went off, a friendship expiration date slip to help me remember, or even have to publicly tell them I'd outgrown them; life had a way of revealing and handling it for me. I realized that as I moved along

41

in life, some friends remained stuck where the old me used to be, and they had no interest in moving anywhere in life. There were other friends who never came down to my level to help pick me back up when I was really down; they never showed me the same amount of loyalty that I always showed them. When things went right with my career, school, or relationship, there were friends who became jealous of my success, turning left in their actions. They truly could not be happy for me because they weren't happy in their own lives. There were also those friendships that made ME go left and leave course, simply because my friends couldn't get it right, and I somehow was swept in. You know, the friend who is best friends with your toxic ex, so every time you get together you also have to see your ex from hell. (By the way, this is a recipe for disaster and also disrespects the new you and/or your new relationship status.) If you want to better your life, you have to outgrow these friendships and surround yourself with people who will help you grow into the person you are meant to be.

Now What?

If a friendship is meant to be outgrown, it will happen organically. The only reason many outgrown relationships stay around so long is that you keep stepping in the way of it, trying to save what's barely there. You see the signs that it's time to let go, but you try to ignore them, as you continue to tell yourself they didn't mean that backhanded comment, they're just going through

43

some personal issues. They don't seem to be calling much ever since you got that new job.. or since your new relationship has become serious. You eventually realize your lives have moved in different directions and hope they will understand and not be mad at you. Stop saving what is no longer meant to be there. A real friend (what I like to call *long term friendships*), will be happy for you despite whatever is going on in anyone's personal life. These friends will be there to support you even if they are not able to be there personally. However, an outgrown friend cannot be happy or support you, because they aren't meant to be there for the long run. Let your friends' actions help you determine who you've outgrown and who is long term. Don't get stuck in the blockage of trying to save an outgrown friendship.

Go Time!

Though outgrowing a friendship hurts, you are actually saving yourself from more pain. Keeping a friend around who's only meant for a season could ultimately make you bitter and act out of character. It may make you regret having given so much love to someone who didn't deserve it; someone who may potentially prevent you from wanting to establishing new relationships with people who are meant to be in your life long term. Keeping it all the way real, having seasonal friends around may destroy your trust in people. Old baggage only holds you down and blocks growth. You can keep the good memories but don't forget the bad ones that helped you make your decision to let that shit go. It will help you realize a lot faster

who else needs to get the hell on.

From the Girls Next Door: *Is He Too Good to Be True?*

I have definitely had my share of heartbreaks. In fact, there came a point when I actually gave up on love. I gave up on love because I felt like I kept getting it wrong. It always started off so great and then ended with me lost, confused, and hurt. I eventually became tired of trying. Then, one day I decided to give it to God. I began to pray for the kind of man I wanted. I became more specific in my prayers, and God finally answered them.

I instantly clicked with this new guy; the chemistry was real, and I was genuinely happy. I noticed how much attention he paid me, how much he made me laugh, and how ambitious he was. He actually wanted to go on real dates, not Netflix and Chill. He appeared to be a man of his word, he was family-oriented, ANDDDDD he was God fearing. So, if he was this perfect, why was I hesitant to move forward?

Have you ever found that perfect someone, only to then start asking yourself: "Is he too good to be true?" It felt so right that it appeared to be scary. I started to question my own prayers. What a bad habit many of us tend to have.

Time to Speak the Truth:

For the first few months of dating this guy, I felt like there had to be a catch. It just seemed too good to be true. He "claimed" to not have any kids, so I *really* thought he was too good to be true! To be totally honest, I was patiently waiting for him to tell me that he had a baby on the way 'but wasn't with the girl anymore' or that he was getting back with his ex; I expected some girl to send me a DM telling me that he was HER man. I couldn't seem to keep myself from remaining a little guarded, just in case one of the stories in my head turned out to be true. Slick things sometimes came out of my mouth because of my fear that something wasn't right. I even practiced scenarios in my head of how I would handle the situation of learning 'the truth' if and when the time came. (I know I am not the only crazy one out there who has done this!) I was not allowing our relationship to flourish. While I waited for him to show his true colors, he continued to show me how great a man he was. Part of me still wanted to run far away, because my feelings were getting deep, and I wanted to avoid having my heart broken. But there was a part of me that wanted to stay, to see if he was really the man I had been praying for.

Now What?

I went to God about this one (forgetting that I had originally gone to Him). I asked God to reveal this man's true colors. I asked God to reveal everything to me that I might need to know. I even asked that God wouldn't allow me to ignore any signs that would be revealed to me -- as people often do. I was basically asking God to show me that He is real. I was questioning the God I put so much faith in. And God answered my prayer, revealing that He had blessed me with the man I had been praying for. God also revealed that he had to wait for me to be in the right place to have that prayer answered; not in a space where I was still caught up in wondering what my ex was doing; not in a space where I was still trying to figure out who I was. God wanted me in a space where I would not take a good man for granted. God also made sure that I understood never to question Him again.

Go Time!

I almost lost someone good because of my past experiences. I had been thinking I wasn't good enough because past relationships made me feel that way. I almost lost someone wonderful because of my slick mouth. Honestly, my words were a cover for the insecurities I was covering up. I had to remember that once I included God in my decision, I would be okay. In fact, I would be more than okay. But let me be the first to say that not everything has been peachy and creamy. Yes, we have our disagreements here and there. Despite them, however, I remain happy. I don't know what the future holds, but what I do know is that this man has definitely raised the bar.

Don't miss out on an opportunity for true love out of fear. Remember, your past is not your present. And, don't go after a person just so you can say you found love. Everyone deserves true love and happiness. Just be sure it's real before you go after it. It's okay to be cautious; but don't be blinded. And most importantly, believe in the power of your own prayer. (Oh, and so far, I've still not been contacted by any baby mamas!)

From the Girls Next Door: *I'm My Own Competition*

YOU know that feeling. You're pretty content with your life. Maybe you're single.. or in a relationship. You may have your dream job.. or at least a job that pays the bills. Maybe you get to travel to your local beach.. or maybe around the world. Whatever your situation is, you're feeling good about your life. Then that thing called *social media* happens. You start scrolling, and your contentedness disappears, giving way to dissatisfied feelings, or maybe even depressed feelings. You've suddenly gone from happy to be alive to unhappy and ungrateful for everything you have in life. Your emotions have done an about face, because you've begun to compare yourself to others.

Time to Speak the Truth:

You were just living your best single life; living well with enough money to pay the bills and even save a little. Then you read about that proposal.. the one you always secretly dreamed of. That couple just looks so happy.. . Their relationship could be a fairytale movie. Did he really just buy her a new car? Oh shit! He bought her a Range Rover. Some dudes won't even volunteer to take their girls' cars to the car wash. You just don't know where these chicks on social media are finding guys that are so in love with them; and buy them CARS! Here you are, just sitting pretty. And sitting single. On your way to your third wedding of the year. You keep catching the damn bouquet, but still can't find *the one*. Who's your best relationship been with? You're favorite bottle of wine, THAT's who. And let's not even talk about all those Instagram pages that post the cutest babies. All you can think about is, "Who will be the father of MY baby?" Oh, and what about all of these self-made millionaires? I can barely afford my monthly gym payments. I just don't get it. What am I doing wrong?

Now What?

Being in this space is not fun. Actually, it's draining. This space will have you confused about what you really want or what you think you may want based on what you see on social media. Unfortunately, everything that glitters is not gold.

Social media is not as real as it appears. I am not saying everyone is lying, because some people's truth is what you see. However, I will say there are a lot of liars out there. It's not your job to determine who may be lying or telling the truth, but it is your job to realize what you want YOUR truth to be. If they deleted all social media tomorrow, would you still want the things you think you want? Would certain things still be important to you? Let's be honest. There are people out there who wouldn't be nearly as excited about the places they go or the things they have if they couldn't post about it all on social media. Take a moment to figure out what YOU genuinely want; not the person you identify yourself as on social media. When you get to the point where you're comparing your life to the lives of other people on social media, you're left with three choices: you can take a break from social media and focus on yourself, use social media as motivation, or continue to be miserable.

Go Time!

Being miserable is not an option. I hate that I even had to mention it. However, the reality is that many people choose to take that option every day. Stop allowing yourself to get caught up in someone else's "reality." Create your own reality, and fall in love with the reality you create! What is meant for you will happen for you. When you become overly invested in someone else's life through social media, you need to take a break from it, for the sake of your own sanity. The time and energy you're putting into scrolling your timeline is the same time and energy that you could be putting into setting and accomplishing your life goals; working on that million-dollar business plan; working on becoming a person who is mentally and emotionally ready for a relationship; working on being better than who you were last year. Compete with yourself. When you compete with yourself, you're guaranteed to win. Comparison is the thief of joy, and you should never allow anyone or anything to steal your joy.

From the Girls Next Door: *I Still Love Him, Even Though I Know I Shouldn't*

Many of us have been in a toxic relationship. That relationship that has caused us so much pain. That relationship that have been so painful, that your loved ones even feel your pain. Although it is so painful, you can't shake the off the love you have that person. It is something about that person you just can't seem to let go. You think the love you have for that person outweighs the pain they are causing you.

Time to Speak the Truth:

You know you are not genuinely happy. You know you have countless nights that you cried yourself to sleep. Situations have occurred in your relationship that is so embarrassing that you haven't even told anyone. The sad truth is that when things are bad, they are bad. However, when things are good, they are great. So, you hold on to the great times hoping they those great times will become consistent. Deep down you know things will not get better, that is why you left.

Now what?

You still find ways to communicate with this person, because you are holding onto that hopeful love. You are still checking their social media from your friend's account or fake page, because you blocked him. You still call their little sister and mother because you still want to be the one the family likes. You are waiting for them to realize you are the one that got away. You hope

this breakup is the one that scares them, even

though this is 313th time you are done with them.

It looks promising this time, because you actually

blocked them from your phone this time. Not only

did you block them, you have ignored them for a

whole more; longer than you ever ignored them

for. You are tired of looking "stupid" and want

your friends to see you are serious this time.

However, you about to unblock them. You need

closure. You need answers to the why and how.

Go Time!

Don't you dare unblock that number. I will

never tell you people do not change. I will tell you

it is rare that people will change in a month. If you

have to be embarrassed about loving a person, they are not for you. Let's just say they did change, you are not ready to be with them. You have suffered in that relationship for so long that you would not be able to recognize the change the person has made. A toxic relationship will cause you to lose yourself. Use this breakup to focus on you. Get you back together. Spend time with you and learn how to love you. Begin to love you so much that you won't accept another topic. Love you much that you don't need to check their social media page. Become so worried about yourself that you do not have time to worry out them...out of sight out of mind. You are always a priority, never an option.

From the Girls Next Door: *I Have a Whole Family, Yet You Are Big Mad That I Don't Have Time*

Have you ever had friends and/or family try to make you feel bad because your life priorities are different from theirs? For example, you have a family (children, boyfriend, fiancé, or husband and children) and your single friends constantly complain that you've changed or that you no longer have any time for them. They keep reminding you that the 'old you' would never miss this or that. They give you a face when you say, "I'm sorry, but I can't make it to that birthday dinner on Friday; I'm just too tired after working all week and helping my kids with their homework." They start to act distant and roll their

63

eyes when you share all that you have going on, and sometimes they have the audacity to send a text message venting about how they feel. You have a family to take care of, and they are mad that you don't have time for them. Now, ain't that some shit?

Time to Speak the Truth:

Single people who behave this way get on my damn nerves because they don't care to understand. They don't care enough to consider that their comments make you feel small, that you somehow lost yourself just because you can't or don't feel like going out on weekends. I used to feel bad when my single friends would gang up on me. I'll never forget the time that I couldn't go to a Halloween birthday party because I had to take my child trick-or-treating instead, and my single friends made me feel horrible. The birthday girl made comments like, "Omg, can't you just trick-or-treat for one hour and then drop her off with a sitter so you can come out for my birthday"? Of course, my other friends chimed in with laughter. I felt like a bad friend in that moment. I tried to think of what I could do to be both a great mom and a good friend but, in the end, I sent that friend a text saying, "I'm sorry. I won't be able to make it." Honestly, I didn't want to go out for her birthday. I wanted to be a mother and take my child trick-or-treating, and come home to watch Halloween movies with her while she went sugar crazy in her costume. That friend didn't talk to me for two days. She didn't understand that she was making me choose between being a good mother or being a good friend. When I chose to be a good mother, she selfishly made the decision that I was being a bad friend. It wasn't until she had a child of her own that she realized the type of choice she had put on me, but I don't think she'll ever understand how that made me feel as her friend.

Single friends are not the only people who put a guilt trip on you when you cannot attend something because you have a family of your own now. Family members will throw salt from time to time, too. I've had family members become upset with me because I missed their calls, or it took me three days to call them back. Hell, after working a full-time job, going to school for my Ph.D., and running two personal businesses, sometimes I just want to cook dinner for my family and relax. After helping with homework, dinner, family check-in on our days, baths, and alone time with my man, I don't feel like talking on the phone. I just recently started making myself squeeze mental time in for my own thoughts/journal time, because once I walk through the door my priority is my own family. I'll never forget the time a family member tried to check me on not being able to make brunch with her and another family member during the time frame she had chosen. Sis, I didn't really even feel bad that I couldn't make it, but I damn sure was pissed that as family who knew me and my situation, they couldn't understand that my schedule was very different from their schedule (i.e.- one of them has a family but doesn't work and the other is single with no kids). I did call and let them both know how they had made me feel, but like my Halloween birthday party friend, I still don't know if they truly understood.

Now What?

People only understand from their own level of perception. You have a family, and so to hell with anyone who is big mad that you do not have time. To be fair, not every friend or family member will act like this. I have single friends who truly understand my life and don't not get mad if I have to reschedule a dinner date. They simply say, "Let me know when you **are** free, and I'll work around you." There are others who say, "Hey, I'll come over to your house with some wine and dinner." Those people I cherish so much because they don't make me feel bad for having a family. They don't stop speaking to me or try to check me because I am too tired to go out when they want me to. So, because of them, I've learned to ignore the people who do try to make me feel bad. If they really cared about me, they wouldn't want to make me feel bad about myself, or imply that I'm a bad friend simply because my priorities are different from theirs at this time in my life.

Go Time!

Do not feel bad for doing what is right. There is nothing wrong with putting your own family ahead of others. Your family is your safe space, and you must give full energy to that. Everyone else comes after. So, if you can make that birthday dinner or brunch with no issues, no pushing your little family to the side, then go, Sis, and have a good time. But if you want to lay on your couch snuggled up with your man watching a good movie or take your kids to the park instead of hanging out with others, then do that, Sis, and have a good time. Those who matter will understand; and those who do not understand, do not matter.

From the Girls Next Door: *How Will the Morning Determine My Day, and Eventually My Life....*

Have you ever had a morning where you are in your panties rumbling through clean clothes (that you still have not folded) trying to find something to wear? Well if you are like me, this has happened plenty of times. Figuring out what I am going to wear with a bonnet full of smashed up curly hair that might act right today (I swear hair has a mind of its own when you have to go somewhere). This morning is a result of my last night. You know the night before where you either had to work late, finish a paper for an extra ass teacher, put the kids to bed, clean the house in order to find that other shoe or expensive ass lipstick; or could not shut your brain off from thinking how to quit the job you have to wake up for in the morning. Those "type" of nights always set us up for an unprepared morning. An unprepared morning feeling so damn unprepared for the day. But wait, what if those unprepared mornings are teaching you a prepared lesson?

Time to Speak the Truth:

I know you are probably thinking, "how does an unprepared morning prepare me for life". I too, questioned myself at first. It took for me to sit down and really think to grasp the concept. An unprepared morning provides a prepared lesson of organization, faith, or taking time for self-care to allow times for your mind to freely think. If we look at those unprepared mornings as day ruiners, do we ever reflect on what to do differently the next time? Unprepared mornings send a cognitive trigger that makes us instantly reflect to the past on how did we end up so damn unprepared. In that moment of self-reflect, an individual can choose to either blame the night before for being unprepared in the morning; or that individual can learn from his or her mistakes from the night before in order to be prepared for the next day.

Now what?

Follow the three P's the night before: *plan, prepare, and pause.* Make a *plan* for everything. Whether you have a big project coming up or thinking of starting a business, planning will help put your ideas into action. Even if an idea is incomplete, writing down your idea on paper is creating a piece to your plan. Great planning activities are creating a goal checklist or vision board. ***Prepare*** yourself for moments of happiness and failures. Sometimes failure will keep you up all night, only for an unprepared morning to come rolling in the next day ready to piss you the hell off even more. Prepare yourself for moments of defeat, so that you can dust your shoulders off, shower away your sorrows, and iron your clothes for the next day. Last but not least, **PAUSE**. In this moment take time to freely think of everything that is going right. Take this moment to pause in gratitude that tomorrow is a new day for you to plan and prepare on how to get closer to your dreams. So often do we forget to pause and be grateful. I'm serious Sis, let that shit go and pause! You still have tomorrow!

Go Time!

If an individual chooses to blame circumstances for being unprepared, that individual has allowed an unprepared morning to negatively condition him or her to use "blaming" as a scapegoat in life. However, if that individual can learn from his or her mistakes, an unprepared morning has positively conditioned him or her to plan and organize better the night before. How we view life situations, such as unprepared mornings, ultimately condition how we view life. Do you want to blame your way through life, or learn from your mistakes?

From the Girls Next Door: *Dealing with Childhood Trauma That Affects You (or Someone in Your Life) As an Adult*

It was not until I became a therapist that I realized my own childhood traumas had been fucking up my life for some time. I know that sentence came on strong; but that is how I felt when I cried to myself, once I realized that all my past memories were not just memories. They continued to live on in the little things I did as an adult. I became aware that although I had grown older in years, I had not outgrown the hurt I had endured.

Time to Speak the Truth:

Sexual abuse, divorce, and seeing domestic violence as a child were my childhood traumas.

When I was six, I was sexually touched by an older cousin on my father's side. I never told anyone as a child because I was so confused as to what had happened to me. When I became a teenager, I still could not tell anyone because I knew my mother would dramatize the situation and my father might kill him. Ironically, my abuser ended up having to go to jail for some other crime, and I never had to see him again. He was out of sight, and I thought, out of mind. However, the trauma was still there. I could never fully trust any man with whom I shared a relationship. I felt like the man had a hidden motive, and eventually would hurt me. So, I would be the one to hurt him first. My sexual abuse left me hurt by a man, and I took that hurt out on other men. It wasn't until I confided in the man who is now my husband and shared the story of my experience with him, that I was able to see how I had allowed my trauma to affect my love life. The trauma had affected my trust.

Even now, as a mother, I never trust my child being alone with anyone. I only allow people with whom I am very close to babysit her; and even then, I ask them to send me pictures and randomly facetime with them to make sure she's safe. When we're at family functions, she's never out of my eye sight for long. I check on her while she is playing just to assure myself that she's okay, because I was touched during a family function during which the adults let the kids go and play. I was able to restore my trust when it came to my love life, but I don't know if I will ever resolve my trust issues when it comes to the safety of my own child. The trauma is just that deep.

Experiencing my parents' divorce and witnessing the domestic violence between my mother and stepfather destroyed my interest in marriage. I had such a distorted vision of what marriage was like that I could say without hesitation that I would never get married. I didn't see any point in making a legal commitment to a relationship that would probably end in divorce anyway. My husband and I were together for 12 years before I finally changed my mind and married him in 2017. It took for him to love me past my trauma for me to be able to take that step. Most importantly, it took for me to allow him to love me past my trauma. I slowly began to understand that my past trauma could only define my present and future if I allowed it to. It was up to me to end the cycle of trauma.

Now What?

Dealing with childhood trauma is difficult. To be honest, it was even difficult for me to write about my experience in this chapter. If I wasn't 6 months pregnant, I would go sip on a drink and woosah right now. Realizing the grip that trauma has on your life, and then finally releasing it, is incredibly hard, but it's absolutely necessary in order for you to grow. You cannot plant new flowers among old existing weeds and expect them to flourish to their full potential of beauty. Pull those weeds out! Bloom into the person you are meant to be, without the trauma camouflaging who you really are or causing even you to believe that you're something/someone else. Counseling helped me. Talking about my trauma helped me. Demanding and then believing that my childhood trauma would no longer define or affect me as an adult is what saved me.

Go Time!

Whether you were sexually or physically abused, grew up without your mother or father, were adopted, were homeless, came from a broken home, or were not loved the way that you should have been as a child.. it is time to heal. Your trauma will only grow if you allow it. The trauma cycle ends when you let it go. Let's heal together, Sis.

From the Girls Next Door: *Being an Entrepreneur is Hard*

Being an entrepreneur IS hard! I know, you probably thought I was going to start that sentence differently, by stating that being an entrepreneur is the best thing ever. You're right; it's that, too. It's a wonderful feeling to accomplish the dream of having your own business. Being an entrepreneur is totally worth the effort; however, it is still as hard as hell.

Time to Speak the Truth:

So, let me explain why I say that being your own boss is hard, especially when the statement "your own boss" sounds so damn good. Being your own boss requires you to be totally honest with yourself. Being an entrepreneur requires you to stop hiding behind the notion that you have it all together. You will have to forcefully tell yourself to stop procrastinating when you're mindlessly scrolling on social media, knowing full well that you should be working on your business plan. You have to continuously motivate yourself and guard against laziness if you expect to create a goal list and follow through with it so that your business will thrive. Yes, it's very easy to say you want to be an entrepreneur, but you cannot be an entrepreneur with old habits. You cannot be an entrepreneur when you still haven't registered your business after a full year of telling yourself you would. Hell, if you haven't managed to create a vision for your brand, come up with a realistic plan for how your business will operate or do the paperwork required to get it started, how do you expect to motivate yourself when you get to the more difficult steps, like getting together the money you'll need for this endeavor? You have to fully realize and accept that being an entrepreneur is hard, and then commit to doing whatever it takes to make your vision a reality.

Now What?

Create a business plan and stick to it. If you want to quit your 9 to 5 job to run your own business, then give yourself a timeline for making that happen. For example, if you want to quit your 9 to 5 to focus on opening your business within one year, then create a savings plan so that you'll be able to pay your bills during that year by putting a certain amount in your saving account each pay period. For me, I put a large amount of my paycheck into savings each month and told myself it was a bill to make sure I consistently did it. Yes, there were times when I looked at that money thinking, "Hmm.. I could use that for a trip somewhere.." but I desperately wanted to get the hell away from my 9 to 5, so I reminded myself that I needed to invest in my business for that to happen. Every time I deposited that large sum into my savings, I left feeling that I was getting closer to my dream. You need to think of ways your new business can create a cash flow as soon as possible after you quit your 9 to 5. This will bring continuous income to your account, and as you grow your business, that income amount will become larger. If you're worried about insurance issues, look into the different healthcare options for those self-employed. Last but not least, remind yourself why you are doing it. For myself, I had three reasons. The first reason was that I wanted to accomplish my dreams, and I knew it if I did that, I would help other people do the same. The second reason was my family. I wanted the freedom to create my own schedule, to be the present mother and wife that I wanted to be. The third reason was because my 9 to 5 was sucking the purpose out of me like a mosquito and no one there gave a damn about me as an employee. While pregnant with my second child, I was so sick that I had to call my supervisor to let him know I wouldn't be in. He never said, "I hope you feel better" or "Take care of yourself." I simply got no response. The next day when I returned, several people came to me with work they needed me to do, but no one asked how I was feeling. That moment was the cherry on top of so many other scoops of moments in which that job made me feel less than appreciated. And that is what motivated me to do whatever it took to get out of there and achieve my own dream of being an entrepreneur, no matter HOW hard it was.

Go Time!

So, you know it's hard to be an entrepreneur, but you also see that it's worth it. Even if you like your 9 to 5, maybe you want to leave something of your own for the generations after you. Trust that that company you're working for won't save a spot for your great grandchildren. However, if you have created your own business, you have also created the potential to leave a

legacy behind and build generational wealth for

your family. So even though starting a business as

an entrepreneur won't be rainbows and glitter, it

will very well may be a gold mine for the future. It

is worth it! Yes, it's hard, but it's SO worth it.

Make a plan and become an entrepreneur, Sis!

From the Girls Next Door: *Am I The Girl That Will Always Be Cheated On?*

Being cheated on sucks. It creates a nauseous pain within in your stomach and confused thoughts in your mind. Hell, that shit hurts your heart! Being cheated on affects your self-esteem, and will have you questioning what did you do wrong. You start to wonder did I give my all or was I good enough? Hell, not to mention the infamous feeling of feeling STUPID pops in your mind from time to time to remind you that this m*therfucker played you. *sigh*. Being cheated on freaking sucks. I too, once wonder am I the girl that will always be cheated on?

Time to Speak the Truth:

89

We have all been there Sis. We have all felt that feeling. If a woman tells you she never been cheated on, either she is lying or hell her man was good as hell hiding it from her ass (kayne shrug) but every woman has definitely been cheated on (don't challenge me, challenge your mother). The feeling sucks and it creates irrational thoughts within your mind on who you are as a woman. But what if I told you that those sucky ass feelings of being cheated on could be turned into self-empowerment nuggets for you to remember who the hell you are! To remind you that you are a woman designed with strength and wisdom! Sis, take that loss and turn it into a lesson! A lesson on what you WILL NOT put up with the next time.

Hell, let that situation be a reason you raise your bar for the next person, or even the same person.

Now what?

For some women you need this moment of being cheated on before you lower your panties to the next one. Seriously Sis, half of the time we get cheated on because we neglected to look at the signs before. Take time to get to know a person before jumping into a relationship with them. He does not have to meet ALL of your standards, but hell he should meet half.

Now do not get me wrong, sometimes there are no signs at all and that shit just comes out of the blue (testimony right here *raises hand*). But use this moment to be smarter. If you decide to give the same man a chance, this will help you lay down some concrete boundaries to remind him who the hell you are, and if he wants this relationship to work being faithful, honest, and committed are main components within the relationship that you should not have to question. As you can see, I am not the type to tell you to immediately walk away after being cheated on. Sometimes individuals grow from a situation after realizing that their actions hurt the one that they love. From a personal standpoint, if I would have completely walked away from my spouse when he cheated, I would not be married today. People do change for the better. HOWEVER, if he keeps cheating, let his ass go Sis.

Go Time!

All in all, do not use that moment of being

cheated on soaking in self-pity or self-doubt, wondering if this is going to be forever. Use that moment of being cheated on to tell yourself that I AM ENOUGH! I am more than enough! So, will you be the girl that will always be cheated on? Hell No! Because every loss is a lesson for you to learn who the hell you are, and what you will not settle for!

From the Girls Next Door: *Self-Empowerment --*
Leap of Faith

"Leap of faith." I don't know why this phrase gives me chills and instantly sends me go into deep thought. For me, leap of faith applies to a number of things in my life. Marriage, career, being a parent, buying a house, starting a business. Hell, sometimes even trying a new hobby feels like a leap of faith. To be honest, writing this book was a leap of faith. My definition of a leap of faith is accepting change in the midst of not knowing how things may turn out. Sounds scary as hell, right?

Time to Speak the Truth:

To some, "leap of faith" may not sound scary, and embracing something new may actually make their adrenaline pump to an exhilarating rate.

However, for me, although I love something new, I actually get nervous as hell when thinking about the "what ifs." What if everything doesn't go as I planned? What if I fail? If I regret this leap, what will other people think about me when I have to start over? These apprehensive questions have led me to sometimes put on snail shoes and move at a slower pace toward fulfilling that "leap" that I so desperately need and subconsciously want to take. I start to feel unmotivated and find my "to do" list piling up with nothing checked off. Those apprehensive questions become momentary roadblocks. It isn't until I realize that I am actually self-sabotaging myself with fear that I realize I need to shake it off and get my shit together.

Now What?

Fear. Fear is the foundation of those apprehensive questions, snail shoes, and self-sabotaging road blocks. Fear is what makes the "what-ifs" feel more real. It is weirdly ironic that when we realize fear is holding us back from taking that leap of faith, we oddly don't feel as afraid anymore. It's like we start to measure up the fear within ourselves and realize we can actually overcome it. We feel silly for being so afraid, and discover we can control our fear. We're able to switch the fear button on and off because fear is simply a thought that we've created within our mind. So, now that you know you have power over fear, what do you plan to do with that power?

Go Time!

No more living in fear. Yes, taking a leap of faith is scary, but living in fear for the rest of your life is much worse. Once you allow fear to dictate a decision within your life, you're at risk of allowing it to control every decision in your life. Next thing you know you'll be living a complacent life with a bunch of shoulda, coulda, wouldas, watching life pass you by because you were too dang afraid to leap. Do not live like that, Sis. I say this from personal experience, as a woman who has taken many leaps of faith within her life, despite her fear. I can honestly say that taking a leap of faith is scary, but it is so worth it. Yes, you may fall; but what if you do not fall and everything actually works out exactly how you hoped for it to be? What if you soar?!

From the Girls Next Door: *Do You Cheer for Yourself as Loud as Others Cheer for You?*

It is such an amazing feeling to have so many people rooting for. Some people would love to receive a quarter support of what you are receiving. In fact, some people feel like the only thing missing is that support from others. On contrary, you have all the support you need, but something is missing. The support from within you is missing. It is not that you don't believe in yourself....or is it?

Time to Speak the Truth:

Some days you are filled with determination, and also feel a bit accomplished. Then there are days you feel like you should have accomplished much more than you have already have. You feel like things are not moving as fast as you would like it to move. These feelings have been arising more often than usual. Part of the reason the feelings are coming more often, is because you keep these feelings hidden from the world. How can you express these feelings when you have so many people rooting for you, praising you, idolizing you, and telling you how proud you make them? So, you just have to play along and fake like you are proud of you. No one wants to feel like they do not believe in themselves. No one wants to be filled with doubt. Doubt tends to play with your self-esteem. Once that is down, everything else can come down with it.

Now what?

You are tired of feeling this way, but don't know how to shake it. You are ready to fight through, but don't know where to begin. The first thing is recognizing you are not alone. Some people may still be in denial, but I want to tell you that I can relate to these haunting feelings. Whenever these feelings arise, I think about every little thing I have accomplished, and how far I have come. Sometimes I laugh thinking about who I was five to ten years ago. My maturity alone is accomplishment. How I handle situations now compared to how I would have handled them before is an accomplishment. Learning new things about me is an accomplishment. I may not be where I want to be, but I am definitely not where I once was. Even if you feel like you are going backwards, take this time to figure out how can you profit from this situation; whether you profit from it financially, emotionally, or even spiritually.

Go Time!

Do NOT wait for everything to go right to cheer for yourself. Cheer for you no matter the circumstances. If the cheering is this loud from others, just imagine how much noise you can make if you joined your support system and cheered for you right along with them. Here's the thing.........if people stop cheering for you, and you are not cheering for yourself, then what?!? You should always be your biggest fan! Now go be proud of you, and keep doing the damn thing!

From the Girls Next Door: *Closure is Not a Necessity*

It is such an annoying feeling to have unanswered questions; especially the infamous "why" questions. You want to know why you were hurt, why you were lied to, why the promises made to you were broken. Why, why, why. My question to you is, WHY do you need those questions answered if you are done? Done for REAL this time? You know, THAT done. The one where you call all your friends and say, "It's DONE." The done where you delete his number and erase all his texts from your phone. The done where you delete all his pictures from social media. Despite all of that, you also know you just want that one last conversation; that closure conversation.

Time to Speak the Truth:

The truth is, you did all of that for no reason, because you are really NOT done. You are not ready to be done if you are still searching for closure. Closure is just an excuse to have another conversation with this person. Closure is a strategy you are using to get your ego stroked, to help increase that self-esteem you lost while you were with him. You want him to tell you the problem is him and not you; how sorry he is that he hurt you; how you're the best person to ever come into his life; how much he loves you; and that he won't do it again. My question to you is, how many times have you heard this before? Once he's said all of that, and answered the questions you've prepared for this "closure conversation," then what? (I'll wait.) NOTHING is going to happen. You know

why? Nothing is going to happen because you

already know the answers to your questions.

You're just not ready to accept the answers

because the answers are the truth, and the truth

hurts.

Now What?

Remember, people only do what you allow

them to do to you. I will never tell anyone what to

do with his or her relationship. Whether it is a

relationship with a friend or a significant other.

What I will tell you, however, is that you don't

ever have to make excuses to communicate with

anyone. You don't need anyone to validate who

you are. You know what you want and what you

deserve. You also know what and who is worth the

fight. AND you know when it's time to break the cycle of going back and forth.

Go Time!

Live your best life! You don't have time to go back and forth with anyone! If the cons outweigh the pros, then it may be time for you to separate yourself from this relationship. If it is meant for the two of you to rekindle that relationship, it will happen after time passes. The closure will come. Life has a way of answering our questions, whether it's in the current moment, next week, or next year. It's up to you to stop being in denial and accept the answers.

From the Girls Next Door: *Where is The Support When You Need It?*

Have you ever felt like you give more support than you receive? It wasn't until I started my own business that I truly saw the real definition of support. I'll never understand how I got 300 likes on a post of me turning up in the club, but somehow only managed to get three likes on me starting a new business. It bothered me that I had more RSVP requests for my birthday parties than I did ticket sales for my first business event. I couldn't wrap my mind around it; and to be quite honest, it hurt my damn feelings.

Time to Speak the Truth:

The truth is that it hurt me. It hurt because I'm the type of person who supports her friends;

whether it's a birthday party, graduation, bar mitzvah, new business opportunity, taking a leap of faith, or moving to a new home. I still contact friends from high school and college to do my hair and lashes, shop at their new boutique, or try out a product they are selling. I do this because I want them to know I'm proud of them and that I'll support them 100%. However, whenever it's been MY turn, that support wasn't reciprocated. Why was it that some of my family members acted like they didn't see my business posts but were somehow always the first to know the new family drama? Why didn't I receive their support? How is it that I have almost a thousand people following me on social media who are friends and family alone, but not even a fraction of those thousand people attend my events? Why do strangers show me more love than my own people do? I just couldn't wrap my mind around it. My hurt was starting to turn into anger, because I wanted the same love that I undeniably gave to others.

Now What?

Now that we've gotten the "I'm pissed that you don't support me" phrase out, let's dig to figure out WHY they don't support me. The number one reason is that they can barely support themselves. It's true. Some people are so unhappy with their own current status in life that there is no way they can muster up space to support your happiness. It's sad, but it's so true. These are the kind of people who would be quick to support you if you wanted to go slash some tires, but who won't help you pass out flyers. The second reason

they don't support you is that some people don't

really want you to make it; they don't see your true

potential. (I know, it's fucked up.) People will

place their own personal fear of not being

successful on you because they can't see it for

themselves. They think your business is

unrealistic, when really, it's about them not

wanting to leave their own reality. The third reason

you don't receive the support you deserve and

expect is that some people think life is a damn

competition. (Ugh. I can't stand these people.)

This last one reminds me of the "crabs in the

bucket" theory. There are folks who think that if

they support you, you are coming for them. When

in truth there is plenty out here for everyone; even

more so because their support *for* you would result in them receiving the same level of support *from* you. What they think is a competition actually has the potential to be a beautiful collaboration.

Go Time!

Though it may be hard (I am definitely talking about myself on this one), do not allow the non-support of others make you mad or want to get even by not supporting *them*. Instead, use those moments to help you grow. Use those moments to help you teach the next generation what *not* to do. Even more so, allow those moments to make you work harder in your businesses, because eventually those same people who haven't supported you will be coming around asking for a job or bragging to others how they know you personally (boop boop,

does a long dramatic hair flip).

From the Girls Next Door: *There is a Time and a Place for Everything (Ratchet versus Righteous)*

So, I know a lot of our STEPsisters might be mad at me for this chapter, but look, Sis, we need to talk about it! We have to learn the difference between ratchet versus righteous. For one, I am so damn tired of seeing us look ratchet out there. Most importantly, our children are watching every move we make and, sure enough, following every single one, too. Don't get me wrong, there have been times when I have done some ratchet things, while thinking to myself, "Girl, you know better." But some of those out there don't seem to realize there's a time and a place for everything, and they take it just too damn far at the wrong times. So, let me introduce the idea of a clear boundary line on what is ratchet versus righteous.

Time to Speak the Truth:

Bonnets and pajama pants should not be worn outside of your house. Unless you are getting the mail, there should be no reason to leave your house wearing a bonnet and pajama pants. Number one, it looks like you just rolled out of bed and didn't brush your teeth. Secondly, it's always the old ass pajama pants that seem to be worn out in public. It looks stank, Sis! I can't stand when I see a woman walk into her children's school with a bonnet and pajama pants on. It's embarrassing for her child! Kids are cruel, so while you're thinking, "I don't care what other people think about me," your child certainly does. Children bully other children about their parents. Hell, I know you remember the "yo momma jokes" as a kid. It also makes it look like you don't have shit to do for the rest of the day or that you don't care about your appearance. You're automatically labeled as ratchet and looked down upon by others, especially at your child's school. I know this first hand from working in a school. The moment you are seen looking ratchet at your child's school, there will be teachers who automatically view your child as such. It may not be right, but hell, it's also not right to come out of the house in your night clothes. If you have to take your child to school or run errands but don't have time to fully get yourself together, then put on a hat. A hat can cover up messed hair. Scarves that are nicely wrapped can work also (There are many videos that show you how to tie them nicely). Put

on sweatpants or leggings instead of pajama pants.

If you know your leggings might look

inappropriate in certain settings, then put a sweater

or jacket around your waist.

Pajamas and bonnets are not the only things

that are viewed ratchet as hell. Horrible customer

service and business etiquette can slip to the

ratchet side, also. I know you're probably

thinking, "I don't care what people think about

me," but, Sis, sometimes you need to. Customers

view how you conduct yourself, and they link it to

how you conduct business. Employers will

categorize you by your appearance, and as a result

may place you in a low-level position where you

won't be seen by the public. Your appearance may

also become a factor when decisions are made about promotions. Don't be mad at me for saying these things, Sis. I just want you to be great.

Now What?

You are better than that, Sis! I see more and more of my female students coming to school with bedtime scarves or bonnets on, and not thinking there's a problem with what they're wearing. These young girls actually get an attitude when I ask them to take these items off! Why are they upset? Because they see YOU do it, and so they think it's okay to look like that. You've set the example, and it's not an example that leads to success. I make them take it off, because I don't want them to go out into society thinking that their appearance doesn't matter. I agree that we shouldn't choose our wardrobe to match other people's opinions, but how you dress should show that you respect yourself enough to look decent in public. If we allow the younger members of society to think they don't have to put any effort into how they look when they walk out into the world, then we have failed to provide them with a basic form of self-respect that they need in order to make something of themselves in this world.

The same thing goes for older people who have nasty or rude attitudes when dealing with customer service or operating their own business. What are they teaching the next generation about business etiquette?

Go Time!

We have to do better, y'all. We have a younger generation of girls looking up to us. Not only that, but putting effort into yourself and/or business is essential to your own self-esteem and self-confidence. While on the inside, in your mind, you're thinking, "I don't care what other people think of me," you are actually presenting on the outside that you don't care about yourself.

From the Girls Next Door: *Breaking Bad Habits*

Breaking bad habits can be hard, especially the type of habits that you know need to be broken; like spending money frivolously, picking the wrong type of partner, generational curses, being negative all the time, substance abuse, or being late for everything.

Time to Speak the Truth:

The excuse, "This is me" or "This is how I have always been" can no longer suffice. Broken people and broken habits build broken foundations in life. Spending money with no regard leads to not having savings for future investments or an emergency fund in case something unexpected happens. I used to have the bad habit of spending too much money which I learned from watching people in my family spending beyond their means. I was carrying a generational bad habit. I was left with a whole bunch of material things, and I was broke as hell. I was looking fly but eating off the dollar menu because I had to make it stretch until I got paid again; and then I'd turn around and do the same dumb shit. Being late all the time was also a horrible habit of mine. In fact, I can't lie; I still struggle with this issue. I still have friends who wait to leave their house when meeting me, because they know from past experience that I'll probably be a little late.

Picking the wrong type of partner is another bad habit. Picking different lovers with the same quality is like wearing the same shirt in a different color. It's nothing new. It may look a bit different, but it's still the same thing. Being negative all the time is definitely a bad habit. If the only thing that comes out of your mouth is something negative when you talk to others, then Sis, this is your habit. People with this bad habit are always quick to gossip about something negative in their life or someone else's. They're also the ones who say, "I don't have any friends," or they play the victim in every damn situation. (Can you tell I cannot stand this type of person? *sigh* whew chile). Substance abuse is a serious bad habit, especially if the user has become dependent on drugs, cigarettes, and/or alcohol in order to cope with life. If you can't function throughout the day without a shot in the morning, it's time to ask yourself what you're trying to escape.

Now What?

Broken people and broken habits build broken foundations in life. So, we have to find resolutions to these habits. Saying that, "This is just me" is old as hell. I mean, after a while you have to grow up and sometimes that means changing some things, Sis. Do I still struggle with some of my bad habits? Absolutely! I still get tempted to spend money and go shopping. However, I pay my savings account first. Just because I have it does not mean I have to spend it. If I haven't put money in my savings account and emergency fund, then I can't splurge without feeling remorse. I actually enjoy seeing a large amount of money in the bank more than I like buying new outfits. I feel more accomplished; and

in return, that's what helped me break my bad
habit.

I still go shopping, but knowing I have
money saved up in case I have a car issue or need
to put down a deposit feels so good. Not to
mention, I was tired of carrying that generational
curse. I refuse to be an older person asking a
younger family member to help pay my bills. My
family is big on asking for handouts, but when it's
time for someone to ask for their money back, they
get mad or go missing.

As for being late, the struggle is still real at
times. To help make this bad habit occur less
often, I've put systems in place. I've changed the
clocks in my house to a later time so that I leave
earlier. I set 10 alarms to make it out door! I'm

serious about the alarms; I put labels on the alarms that tell me what I should be doing at a certain time. Some may call this crazy, but I call it self-accountability.

Picking the wrong lover starts from within; you have to change your mindset. The moment you notice the new person you're dating has behaviors that remind you of your ex, then let that person go! You've been down that road before, why travel it again? If you notice qualities in the new person that make you feel uncomfortable, then let that person go. The signs will be there, you just have to learn to break the bad habit of ignoring the signs until it's too late.

Being negative all the time starts from within also. If you notice no one wants to be around you at times or that they're quick to say, "Let me call you back," but they don't, it's because your vibe is off as hell. No one wants to hear a sob story all the damn time. Speaking negatively all the time makes you look negative. If you stop and notice that all you ever have to share is a sob story or something negative about someone else's, then you truly need to break this habit. It strips away your happiness in life and even takes away people who want to care for you but just don't feel like hearing that negativity all the time.

Go Time!

No one is perfect. Everyone has a bad habit or two that need to be broken. Some are listed in this chapter, but there are many others, such as overeating or procrastinating. Whatever bad habit it is that you need to break, ask yourself these three questions:

1. What systems do I have in place that have created this habit?

2. How is this habit affecting my life?

3. What do I need to change internally so that I can break this habit?

I highly recommend talking to a counselor after answering these three questions so that you have an unbiased support system to help you.

Made in the USA
Columbia, SC
06 August 2019